enVisionmath 2.0
SCOTT FORESMAN • ADDISON WESLEY

Volume 1 Topics 1–7

Authors

Randall I. Charles
Professor Emeritus
Department of Mathematics
San Jose State University
San Jose, California

Jennifer Bay-Williams
Professor of Mathematics
Education
College of Education and Human
Development
University of Louisville
Louisville, Kentucky

Robert Q. Berry, III
Associate Professor of
Mathematics Education
Department of Curriculum,
Instruction and Special Education
University of Virginia
Charlottesville, Virginia

Janet H. Caldwell
Professor of Mathematics
Rowan University
Glassboro, New Jersey

Zachary Champagne
Assistant in Research
Florida Center for Research in
Science, Technology, Engineering,
and Mathematics (FCR-STEM)
Jacksonville, Florida

Juanita Copley
Professor Emerita, College of
Education
University of Houston
Houston, Texas

Warren Crown
Professor Emeritus of Mathematics
Education
Graduate School of Education
Rutgers University
New Brunswick, New Jersey

Francis (Skip) Fennell
L. Stanley Bowlsbey Professor
of Education and Graduate and
Professional Studies
McDaniel College
Westminster, Maryland

Karen Karp
Professor of Mathematics
Education
Department of Early Childhood
and Elementary Education
University of Louisville
Louisville, Kentucky

Stuart J. Murphy
Visual Learning Specialist
Boston, Massachusetts

Jane F. Schielack
Professor of Mathematics
Associate Dean for Assessment
and Pre K-12 Education,
College of Science
Texas A&M University
College Station, Texas

Jennifer M. Suh
Associate Professor for
Mathematics Education
George Mason University
Fairfax, Virginia

Jonathan A. Wray
Mathematics Instructional
Facilitator
Howard County Public Schools
Ellicott City, Maryland

Glenview, Illinois   Boston, Massachusetts   Chandler, Arizona   Hoboken, New Jersey

Mathematicians

Roger Howe
Professor of Mathematics
Yale University
New Haven, Connecticut

Gary Lippman
Professor of Mathematics
and Computer Science
California State University,
East Bay
Hayward, California

ELL Consultants

Janice R. Corona
Independent Education
Consultant
Dallas, Texas

Jim Cummins
Professor
The University of Toronto
Toronto, Canada

Common Core State Standards Reviewers

Debbie Crisco
Math Coach
Beebe Public Schools
Beebe, Arkansas

Kathleen A. Cuff
Teacher
Kings Park Central School District
Kings Park, New York

Erika Doyle
Math and Science Coordinator
Richland School District
Richland, Washington

Susan Jarvis
Math and Science Curriculum
Coordinator
Ocean Springs Schools
Ocean Springs, Mississippi

Velvet M. Simington
K-12 Mathematics Director
Winston-Salem / Forsyth County
Schools
Winston-Salem, North Carolina

ISBN-13: 978-0-328-82738-1
ISBN-10: 0-328-82738-X

Digital Resources

Go to PearsonRealize.com

MP

Math Practices Animations to play anytime

Learn

Visual Learning Animation Plus with animation, interaction, and math tools

Practice Buddy

Online Personalized Practice for each lesson

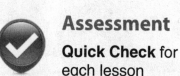

Assessment

Quick Check for each lesson

Games

Math Games to help you learn

ACTIVe-book

Student Edition online for showing your work

Solve

Solve & Share problems plus math tools

Glossary

Animated Glossary in English and Spanish

Tools

Math Tools to help you understand

Help

Another Look Homework Video for extra help

eText

Student Edition online

PEARSON
realize™ Everything you need for math anytime, anywhere

KEY

- ● Major Cluster
- ● Supporting Cluster
- ● Additional Cluster

The content is organized to focus on Common Core clusters.

For a list of clusters, see pages F13–F16.

Digital Resources at PearsonRealize.com

And remember your eText is available at PearsonRealize.com!

Contents

You can represent multiplication as an array with equal rows and columns.

5 columns

4 rows

$$4 \times 5 = 20$$

number of rows

number in each row

TOPIC 1 Understand Multiplication and Division of Whole Numbers

You can use patterns to help remember multiplication facts.

DATA

9s Facts

$0 \times 9 = 0$

$1 \times 9 = 9$

$2 \times 9 = 18$

$3 \times 9 = 27$

$4 \times 9 = 36$

$5 \times 9 = 45$

$6 \times 9 = 54$

$7 \times 9 =$

$8 \times 9 =$

$9 \times 9 =$

TOPIC 2 Multiplication Facts: Use Patterns

Properties can help you use known facts to find unknown facts.

6×4

2×4

4×4

TOPIC 3 Apply Properties: Multiplication Facts for 3, 4, 6, 7, 8

Multiplication facts can help you learn division facts.

Multiplication
3 rows of 10 drums

$3 \times 10 = 30$

30 drums

Division
30 drums in 3 equal rows

$30 \div 3 = 10$

10 drums in each row

TOPIC 4 Use Multiplication to Divide: Division Facts

You can use a multiplication table to find missing factors.

$$3 \times 5 = 15 \qquad 15 \div 3 = 5$$

×	0	1	2	3	4	5
0	0	0	0	0	0	0
1	0	1	2	3	4	5
2	0	2	4	6	8	10
3	0	3	6	9	12	15

TOPIC 5 Fluently Multiply and Divide within 100

> You can find the area of a shape by counting the number of unit squares needed to cover it.

TOPIC 6 Connect Area to Multiplication and Addition

You can use a scaled bar graph to help compare data.

Amount Greg Saved Each Month

TOPIC 7 Represent and Interpret Data

KEY

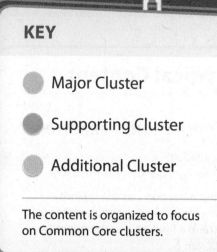

- ● Major Cluster
- ● Supporting Cluster
- ● Additional Cluster

The content is organized to focus on Common Core clusters.

Dear Families,

The standards on the following pages describe the math that students will learn this year. The greatest amount of time will be spent on standards in the major clusters.

Grade 3 Common Core Standards

Common Core Standards for Mathematical Content

DOMAIN 3.OA
OPERATIONS AND ALGEBRAIC THINKING

MAJOR CLUSTER 3.OA.A
Represent and solve problems involving multiplication and division.

3.OA.A.1 Interpret products of whole numbers, e.g., interpret 5×7 as the total number of objects in 5 groups of 7 objects each. *For example, describe a context in which a total number of objects can be expressed as 5×7.*

3.OA.A.2 Interpret whole-number quotients of whole numbers, e.g., interpret $56 \div 8$ as the number of objects in each share when 56 objects are partitioned equally into 8 shares, or as a number of shares when 56 objects are partitioned into equal shares of 8 objects each. *For example, describe a context in which a number of shares or a number of groups can be expressed as $56 \div 8$.*

3.OA.A.3 Use multiplication and division within 100 to solve word problems in situations involving equal groups, arrays, and measurement quantities, e.g., by using drawings and equations with a symbol for the unknown number to represent the problem.

3.OA.A.4 Determine the unknown whole number in a multiplication or division equation relating three whole numbers. *For example, determine the unknown number that makes the equation true in each of the equations $8 \times ? = 48$, $5 = \_\_ \div 3$, $6 \times 6 = ?$*

MAJOR CLUSTER 3.OA.B
Understand properties of multiplication and the relationship between multiplication and division.

3.OA.B.5 Apply properties of operations as strategies to multiply and divide.[1] *Examples: If $6 \times 4 = 24$ is known, then $4 \times 6 = 24$ is also known. (Commutative property of multiplication.) $3 \times 5 \times 2$ can be found by $3 \times 5 = 15$, then $15 \times 2 = 30$, or by $5 \times 2 = 10$, then $3 \times 10 = 30$. (Associative property of multiplication.) Knowing that $8 \times 5 = 40$ and $8 \times 2 = 16$, one can find 8×7 as $8 \times (5 + 2) = (8 \times 5) + (8 \times 2) = 40 + 16 = 56$. (Distributive property.)*

3.OA.B.6 Understand division as an unknown-factor problem. *For example, find $32 \div 8$ by finding the number that makes 32 when multiplied by 8.*

Common Core Standards for Mathematical Content

MAJOR CLUSTER 3.OA.C
Multiply and divide within 100.

3.OA.C.7 Fluently multiply and divide within 100, using strategies such as the relationship between multiplication and division (e.g., knowing that $8 \times 5 = 40$, one knows $40 \div 5 = 8$) or properties of operations. By the end of Grade 3, know from memory all products of two one-digit numbers.

MAJOR CLUSTER 3.OA.D
Solve problems involving the four operations, and identify and explain patterns in arithmetic.

3.OA.D.8 Solve two-step word problems using the four operations. Represent these problems using equations with a letter standing for the unknown quantity. Assess the reasonableness of answers using mental computation and estimation strategies including rounding.[2]

3.OA.D.9 Identify arithmetic patterns (including patterns in the addition table or multiplication table), and explain them using properties of operations. *For example, observe that 4 times a number is always even, and explain why 4 times a number can be decomposed into two equal addends.*

DOMAIN 3.NBT
NUMBER AND OPERATIONS IN BASE TEN

ADDITIONAL CLUSTER 3.NBT.A
Use place value understanding and properties of operations to perform multi-digit arithmetic.[3]

3.NBT.A.1 Use place value understanding to round whole numbers to the nearest 10 or 100.

3.NBT.A.2 Fluently add and subtract within 1000 using strategies and algorithms based on place value, properties of operations, and/or the relationship between addition and subtraction.

3.NBT.A.3 Multiply one-digit whole numbers by multiples of 10 in the range 10-90 (e.g., 9×80, 5×60) using strategies based on place value and properties of operations.

DOMAIN 3.NF
NUMBER AND OPERATIONS – FRACTIONS[4]

MAJOR CLUSTER 3.NF.A
Develop understanding of fractions as numbers.

3.NF.A.1 Understand a fraction $\frac{1}{b}$ as the quantity formed by 1 part when a whole is partitioned into b equal parts; understand a fraction $\frac{a}{b}$ as the quantity formed by a parts of size $\frac{1}{b}$.

3.NF.A.2 Understand a fraction as a number on the number line; represent fractions on a number line diagram.

3.NF.A.2a Represent a fraction $\frac{1}{b}$ on a number line diagram by defining the interval from 0 to 1 as the whole and partitioning it into b equal parts. Recognize that each part has size $\frac{1}{b}$ and that the endpoint of the part based at 0 locates the number $\frac{1}{b}$ on the number line.

3.NF.A.2b Represent a fraction $\frac{a}{b}$ on a number line diagram by marking off a lengths $\frac{1}{b}$ from 0. Recognize that the resulting interval has size $\frac{a}{b}$ and that its endpoint locates the number $\frac{a}{b}$ on the number line.

3.NF.A.3 Explain equivalence of fractions in special cases, and compare fractions by reasoning about their size.

3.NF.A.3a Understand two fractions as equivalent (equal) if they are the same size, or the same point on a number line.

3.NF.A.3b Recognize and generate simple equivalent fractions, e.g., $\frac{1}{2} = \frac{2}{4}$, $\frac{4}{6} = \frac{2}{3}$. Explain why the fractions are equivalent, e.g., by using a visual fraction model.

3.NF.A.3c Express whole numbers as fractions, and recognize fractions that are equivalent to whole numbers. *Examples: Express 3 in the form $3 = \frac{3}{1}$; recognize that $\frac{6}{1} = 6$; locate $\frac{4}{4}$ and 1 at the same point of a number line diagram.*

3.NF.A.3d Compare two fractions with the same numerator or the same denominator by reasoning about their size. Recognize that comparisons are valid only when the two fractions refer to the same whole. Record the results of comparisons with the symbols $>$, $=$, or $<$, and justify the conclusions, e.g., by using a visual fraction model.

Common Core Standards for Mathematical Content

DOMAIN 3.MD
MEASUREMENT AND DATA

MAJOR CLUSTER 3.MD.A
Solve problems involving measurement and estimation of intervals of time, liquid volumes, and masses of objects.

3.MD.A.1 Tell and write time to the nearest minute and measure time intervals in minutes. Solve word problems involving addition and subtraction of time intervals in minutes, e.g., by representing the problem on a number line diagram.

3.MD.A.2 Measure and estimate liquid volumes and masses of objects using standard units of grams (g), kilograms (kg), and liters (l).[5] Add, subtract, multiply, or divide to solve one-step word problems involving masses or volumes that are given in the same units, e.g., by using drawings (such as a beaker with a measurement scale) to represent the problem.[6]

SUPPORTING CLUSTER 3.MD.B
Represent and interpret data.

3.MD.B.3 Draw a scaled picture graph and a scaled bar graph to represent a data set with several categories. Solve one- and two-step "how many more" and "how many less" problems using information presented in scaled bar graphs. *For example, draw a bar graph in which each square in the bar graph might represent 5 pets.*

3.MD.B.4 Generate measurement data by measuring lengths using rulers marked with halves and fourths of an inch. Show the data by making a line plot, where the horizontal scale is marked off in appropriate units— whole numbers, halves, or quarters.

MAJOR CLUSTER 3.MD.C
Geometric measurement: understand concepts of area and relate area to multiplication and to addition.

3.MD.C.5 Recognize area as an attribute of plane figures and understand concepts of area measurement.

3.MD.C.5a A square with side length 1 unit, called "a unit square," is said to have "one square unit" of area, and can be used to measure area.

3.MD.C.5b A plane figure which can be covered without gaps or overlaps by *n* unit squares is said to have an area of *n* square units.

3.MD.C.6 Measure areas by counting unit squares (square cm, square m, square in, square ft, and improvised units).

3.MD.C.7 Relate area to the operations of multiplication and addition.

3.MD.C.7a Find the area of a rectangle with whole-number side lengths by tiling it, and show that the area is the same as would be found by multiplying the side lengths.

3.MD.C.7b Multiply side lengths to find areas of rectangles with whole-number side lengths in the context of solving real world and mathematical problems, and represent whole-number products as rectangular areas in mathematical reasoning.

3.MD.C.7c Use tiling to show in a concrete case that the area of a rectangle with whole-number side lengths a and $b + c$ is the sum of $a \times b$ and $a \times c$. Use area models to represent the distributive property in mathematical reasoning.

3.MD.C.7d Recognize area as additive. Find areas of rectilinear figures by decomposing them into non-overlapping rectangles and adding the areas of the non-overlapping parts, applying this technique to solve real world problems.

ADDITIONAL CLUSTER 3.MD.D
Geometric measurement: recognize perimeter as an attribute of plane figures and distinguish between linear and area measures.

3.MD.D.8 Solve real world and mathematical problems involving perimeters of polygons, including finding the perimeter given the side lengths, finding an unknown side length, and exhibiting rectangles with the same perimeter and different areas or with the same area and different perimeters.

Common Core Standards for Mathematical Content

DOMAIN 3.G
GEOMETRY

SUPPORTING CLUSTER 3.G.A
Reason with shapes and their attributes.

3.G.A.1 Understand that shapes in different categories (e.g., rhombuses, rectangles, and others) may share attributes (e.g., having four sides), and that the shared attributes can define a larger category (e.g., quadrilaterals). Recognize rhombuses, rectangles, and squares as examples of quadrilaterals, and draw examples of quadrilaterals that do not belong to any of these subcategories.

3.G.A.2 Partition shapes into parts with equal areas. Express the area of each part as a unit fraction of the whole. *For example, partition a shape into 4 parts with equal area, and describe the area of each part as $\frac{1}{4}$ of the area of the shape.*

---

[1]Students need not use formal terms for these properties.

[2]This standard is limited to problems posed with whole numbers and having whole-number answers; students should know how to perform operations in the conventional order when there are no parentheses to specify a particular order (Order of Operations).

[3]A range of algorithms may be used.

[4]Grade 3 expectations in this domain are limited to fractions with denominators 2, 3, 4, 6, and 8.

[5]Excludes compound units such as cm^3 and finding the geometric volume of a container.

[6]Excludes multiplicative comparison problems (problems involving notions of "times as much").

Common Core Standards for Mathematical Practice

MP.1 MAKE SENSE OF PROBLEMS AND PERSEVERE IN SOLVING THEM.

Mathematically proficient students start by explaining to themselves the meaning of a problem and looking for entry points to its solution. They analyze givens, constraints, relationships, and goals. They make conjectures about the form and meaning of the solution and plan a solution pathway rather than simply jumping into a solution attempt. They consider analogous problems, and try special cases and simpler forms of the original problem in order to gain insight into its solution. They monitor and evaluate their progress and change course if necessary. Older students might, depending on the context of the problem, transform algebraic expressions or change the viewing window on their graphing calculator to get the information they need. Mathematically proficient students can explain correspondences between equations, verbal descriptions, tables, and graphs or draw diagrams of important features and relationships, graph data, and search for regularity or trends. Younger students might rely on using concrete objects or pictures to help conceptualize and solve a problem. Mathematically proficient students check their answers to problems using a different method, and they continually ask themselves, "Does this make sense?" They can understand the approaches of others to solving complex problems and identify correspondences between different approaches.

MP.2 REASON ABSTRACTLY AND QUANTITATIVELY.

Mathematically proficient students make sense of quantities and their relationships in problem situations. They bring two complementary abilities to bear on problems involving quantitative relationships: the ability to *decontextualize*—to abstract a given situation and represent it symbolically and manipulate the representing symbols as if they have a life of their own, without necessarily attending to their referents—and the ability to *contextualize*, to pause as needed during the manipulation process in order to probe into the referents for the symbols involved. Quantitative reasoning entails habits of creating a coherent representation of the problem at hand; considering the units involved; attending to the meaning of quantities, not just how to compute them; and knowing and flexibly using different properties of operations and objects.

MP.3 CONSTRUCT VIABLE ARGUMENTS AND CRITIQUE THE REASONING OF OTHERS.

Mathematically proficient students understand and use stated assumptions, definitions, and previously established results in constructing arguments. They make conjectures and build a logical progression of statements to explore the truth of their conjectures. They are able to analyze situations by breaking them into cases, and can recognize and use counterexamples. They justify their conclusions, communicate them to others, and respond to the arguments of others. They reason inductively about data, making plausible arguments that take into account the context from which the data arose. Mathematically proficient students are also able to compare the effectiveness of two plausible arguments, distinguish correct logic or reasoning from that which is flawed, and—if there is a flaw in an argument—explain what it is. Elementary students can construct arguments using concrete referents such as objects, drawings, diagrams, and actions. Such arguments can make sense and be correct, even though they are not generalized or made formal until later grades. Later, students learn to determine domains to which an argument applies. Students at all grades can listen to or read the arguments of others, decide whether they make sense, and ask useful questions to clarify or improve the arguments.

MP.4 MODEL WITH MATHEMATICS.

Mathematically proficient students can apply the mathematics they know to solve problems arising in everyday life, society, and the workplace. In early grades, this might be as simple as writing an addition equation to describe a situation. In middle grades, a student might apply proportional reasoning to plan a school event or analyze a problem in the community. By high school, a student might use geometry to solve a design problem or use a function to describe how one quantity of interest depends on another. Mathematically proficient students who can apply what they know are comfortable making assumptions and approximations to simplify a complicated situation, realizing that these may need revision later. They are able to identify important quantities in a practical situation and map their relationships using such tools as diagrams, two-way tables, graphs, flowcharts and formulas. They can analyze those relationships mathematically to draw conclusions. They routinely interpret their mathematical results in the context of the situation and reflect on

Common Core Standards for Mathematical Practice

whether the results make sense, possibly improving the model if it has not served its purpose.

MP.5 USE APPROPRIATE TOOLS STRATEGICALLY.

Mathematically proficient students consider the available tools when solving a mathematical problem. These tools might include pencil and paper, concrete models, a ruler, a protractor, a calculator, a spreadsheet, a computer algebra system, a statistical package, or dynamic geometry software. Proficient students are sufficiently familiar with tools appropriate for their grade or course to make sound decisions about when each of these tools might be helpful, recognizing both the insight to be gained and their limitations. For example, mathematically proficient high school students analyze graphs of functions and solutions generated using a graphing calculator. They detect possible errors by strategically using estimation and other mathematical knowledge. When making mathematical models, they know that technology can enable them to visualize the results of varying assumptions, explore consequences, and compare predictions with data. Mathematically proficient students at various grade levels are able to identify relevant external mathematical resources, such as digital content located on a website, and use them to pose or solve problems. They are able to use technological tools to explore and deepen their understanding of concepts.

MP.6 ATTEND TO PRECISION.

Mathematically proficient students try to communicate precisely to others. They try to use clear definitions in discussion with others and in their own reasoning. They state the meaning of the symbols they choose, including using the equal sign consistently and appropriately. They are careful about specifying units of measure, and labeling axes to clarify the correspondence with quantities in a problem. They calculate accurately and efficiently, express numerical answers with a degree of precision appropriate for the problem context. In the elementary grades, students give carefully formulated explanations to each other. By the time they reach high school they have learned to examine claims and make explicit use of definitions.

MP.7 LOOK FOR AND MAKE USE OF STRUCTURE.

Mathematically proficient students look closely to discern a pattern or structure. Young students, for example, might notice that three and seven more is the same amount as seven and three more, or they may sort a collection of shapes according to how many sides the shapes have. Later, students will see 7×8 equals the well remembered $7 \times 5 + 7 \times 3$, in preparation for learning about the distributive property. In the expression $x^2 + 9x + 14$, older students can see the 14 as 2×7 and the 9 as $2 + 7$. They recognize the significance of an existing line in a geometric figure and can use the strategy of drawing an auxiliary line for solving problems. They also can step back for an overview and shift perspective. They can see complicated things, such as some algebraic expressions, as single objects or as being composed of several objects. For example, they can see $5 - 3(x - y)^2$ as 5 minus a positive number times a square and use that to realize that its value cannot be more than 5 for any real numbers x and y.

MP.8 LOOK FOR AND EXPRESS REGULARITY IN REPEATED REASONING.

Mathematically proficient students notice if calculations are repeated, and look both for general methods and for shortcuts. Upper elementary students might notice when dividing 25 by 11 that they are repeating the same calculations over and over again, and conclude they have a repeating decimal. By paying attention to the calculation of slope as they repeatedly check whether points are on the line through (1, 2) with slope 3, middle school students might abstract the equation $(y - 2)/(x - 1) = 3$. Noticing the regularity in the way terms cancel when expanding $(x - 1)(x + 1)$, $(x - 1)(x^2 + x + 1)$, and $(x - 1)(x^3 + x^2 + x + 1)$ might lead them to the general formula for the sum of a geometric series. As they work to solve a problem, mathematically proficient students maintain oversight of the process, while attending to the details. They continually evaluate the reasonableness of their intermediate results.

Math Practices and Problem Solving Handbook

Math practices are ways we think about and do math.

Math practices help us solve problems.

Math Practices

MP.1 Make sense of problems and persevere in solving them.

MP.2 Reason abstractly and quantitatively.

MP.3 Construct viable arguments and critique the reasoning of others.

MP.4 Model with mathematics.

MP.5 Use appropriate tools strategically.

MP.6 Attend to precision.

MP.7 Look for and make use of structure.

MP.8 Look for and express regularity in repeated reasoning.

There are good Thinking Habits for each of these math practices.

MP.1 Make sense of problems and persevere in solving them.

Good math thinkers make sense of problems and think of ways to solve them.

If they get stuck, they don't give up.

Mia has $36. Kate has $17 less than Mia. Do Mia and Kate together have enough money to buy a bike for $54?

Here I listed what I know and what I am trying to find.

What I Know:
- Mia has $36.
- Kate has $17 less than $36.
- The bike costs $54.

What I need to find:
- Whether Kate and Mia have at least $54 in all.

Thinking Habits

Be a good thinker! These questions can help you.

- What do I need to find?
- What do I know?
- What's my plan for solving the problem?
- What else can I try if I get stuck?
- How can I check that my solution makes sense?

MP.2 Reason abstractly and quantitatively.

Good math thinkers know how to think about words and numbers to solve problems.

I drew a bar diagram that shows how things in the problem are related.

Jake bought a coat for $47. He also bought a shirt. Jake spent $71 in all. How much did he spend on the shirt?

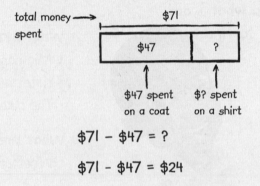

total money spent ——→ $71

$47 | ?

$47 spent on a coat

$? spent on a shirt

$71 − $47 = ?

$71 − $47 = $24

Thinking Habits

Be a good thinker! These questions can help you.

- What do the numbers and symbols in the problem mean?

- How are the numbers or quantities related?

- How can I represent a word problem using pictures, numbers, or equations?

Math Practices and Problem Solving Handbook

MP.3 Construct viable arguments and critique the reasoning of others.

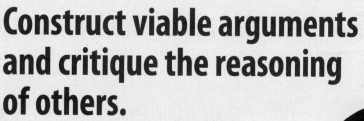

Good math thinkers use math to explain why they are right. They can talk about the math that others do, too.

I wrote a clear argument with words, numbers, and symbols.

Lydia has 3 coins. She has 60¢ in all. Could all of Lydia's coins be quarters? Explain why or why not.

Marta's Work

Lydia's coins cannot all be quarters.
1 quarter is 25¢.
3 quarters is 25¢, 50¢, 75¢.
75¢ > 60¢
So, 3 quarters is more money than Lydia actually has.

Thinking Habits

Be a good thinker! These questions can help you.

- How can I use numbers, objects, drawings, or actions to justify my argument?

- Am I using numbers and symbols correctly?

- Is my explanation clear and complete?

- What questions can I ask to understand other people's thinking?

- Are there mistakes in other people's thinking?

- Can I improve other people's thinking?

MP.4 Model with mathematics.

Good math thinkers choose and apply math they know to show and solve problems from everyday life.

Harry has carrots in his garden. Harry has 5 rows of carrots with 4 carrots in each row. How many carrots are in Harry's garden?

○ ○ ○ ○
○ ○ ○ ○
○ ○ ○ ○
○ ○ ○ ○
○ ○ ○ ○

4 + 4 + 4 + 4 + 4 = 20
There are 20 carrots in Harry's garden.

I used what I know about arrays and addition. I drew a picture to help.

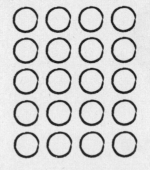

Thinking Habits

Be a good thinker! These questions can help you.

- How can I use math I know to help solve this problem?

- How can I use pictures, objects, or an equation to represent the problem?

- How can I use numbers, words, and symbols to solve the problem?

MP.5 Use appropriate tools strategically.

Good math thinkers know how to pick the right tools to solve math problems.

I decided to use place-value blocks to help me compare. I can use them to show the hundreds, the tens, and the ones.

Carla has 234 stickers. Dan has 242 stickers. Who has more stickers?

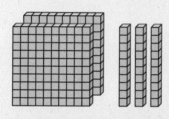 :

242 is greater than 234.
Dan has more stickers.

Thinking Habits

Be a good thinker! These questions can help you.

- Which tools can I use?
- Why should I use this tool to help me solve the problem?
- Is there a different tool I could use?
- Am I using the tool appropriately?

MP.6 Attend to precision.

Good math thinkers are careful about what they write and say, so their ideas about math are clear.

I was precise with my measurements and the way that I wrote my solution.

Which of these two paths is longer? How much longer?

Blue path: 3 cm + 3 cm = 6 cm
Yellow path: 4 cm + 1 cm = 5 cm
6 cm - 5 cm = 1 cm
The blue path is 1 cm longer than the yellow path.

Thinking Habits

Be a good thinker! These questions can help you.

- Am I using numbers, units, and symbols appropriately?

- Am I using the correct definitions?

- Am I calculating accurately?

- Is my answer clear?

MP.7 Look for and make use of structure.

Good math thinkers look for patterns or relationships in math to help solve problems.

I broke apart 67 to solve 123 – 67.

A store has 123 apples. 67 apples are sold. How many apples does the store have left?

123 – 67 = ?

I know 67 = 60 + 7.
123 – 60 = 63
63 – 7 = 56

So, 123 – 67 = 56.
The store has 56 apples left.

Thinking Habits

Be a good thinker! These questions can help you.

- What patterns can I see and describe?

- How can I use the patterns to solve the problem?

- Can I see expressions and objects in different ways?

MP.8 Look for and express regularity in repeated reasoning.

Good math thinkers look for things that repeat, and they make generalizations.

I used reasoning to generalize about calculations.

Find the sum for each of these addends.

$185 + 100 = ?$

$? = 292 + 100$

$100 + 321 = ?$

Daniel's Work

$185 + 100 = 285$

$392 = 292 + 100$

$100 + 321 = 421$

100 is added in each problem.
Adding 100 makes the hundreds digit go up by 1.

Thinking Habits

Be a good thinker! These questions can help you.

- Are any calculations repeated?

- Can I generalize from examples?

- What shortcuts do I notice?

Problem Solving Guide

Math practices can help you solve problems.

Make Sense of the Problem

Reason Abstractly and Quantitatively

- What do I need to find?
- What given information can I use?
- How are the quantities related?

Think About Similar Problems

- Have I solved problems like this before?

Persevere in Solving the Problem

Model with Math

- How can I use the math I know?
- How can I represent the problem?
- Is there a pattern or structure I can use?

Some Ways to Represent Problems

- Draw a Picture
- Make a Bar Diagram
- Make a Table or Graph
- Write an Equation

Use Appropriate Tools Strategically

- What math tools could I use?
- How can I use those tools strategically?

Some Math Tools

- Objects
- Grid Paper
- Rulers
- Technology
- Paper and Pencil

Check the Answer

Make Sense of the Answer

- Is my answer reasonable?

Check for Precision

- Did I check my work?
- Is my answer clear?
- Did I construct a viable argument?
- Did I generalize correctly?

Math Practices and Problem Solving Handbook

Problem Solving Recording Sheet

This sheet helps you organize your work.

Name **Carlos**

Teaching Tool
1

Problem Solving Recording Sheet

Problem:
Cory wants to buy a video game that costs $60. He has $48 saved. On Monday he used part of his savings to buy a shirt for $15. How much more money does Cory need to save to buy the video game?

MAKE SENSE OF THE PROBLEM

Need to Find

Money needed to buy video game

Given

Video game costs $60
Saved $48
Used $15 of savings

PERSEVERE IN SOLVING THE PROBLEM

Some Ways to Represent Problems

☐ Draw a Picture
☑ Make a Bar Diagram
☐ Make a Table or Graph
☐ Write an Equation

Some Math Tools

☐ Objects
☐ Grid Paper
☐ Rulers
☐ Technology
☑ Paper and Pencil

Solution and Answer

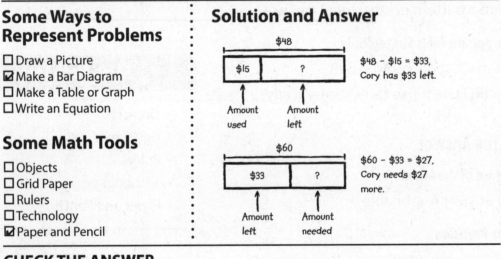

$48 − $15 = $33,
Cory has $33 left.

$60 − $33 = $27,
Cory needs $27 more.

CHECK THE ANSWER

Estimate
50 − 20 = 30   60 − 30 = 30
Check
33 + 15 = 48   27 + 33 = 60

My answer is reasonable and makes sense.
My answer is correct.

T1

Math Practices and Problem Solving Handbook

Bar Diagrams

You can draw a **bar diagram** to show how the quantities in a problem are related. Then you can write an equation to solve the problem.

Add To

Draw this **bar diagram** for situations that involve *adding* to a quantity.

Result →

	82	
15	67	

↑ Start   ↑ Change

Result Unknown

Greg bought a baseball and a baseball glove. How much did he pay for both?

$30

$13

? dollars spent on both →

	?	
13	30	

↑ $13 for baseball   ↑ $30 for baseball glove

$13 + 30 = ?$

Greg spent $43 on both.

Start Unknown

Robin had some rings. Her sister gave her the rings shown below. After that, Robin had 90 rings. How many rings did Robin start with?

90 rings →

	90	
?	34	

↑ ? rings to start   ↑ 34 rings added

$? + 34 = 90$

Robin started with 56 rings.

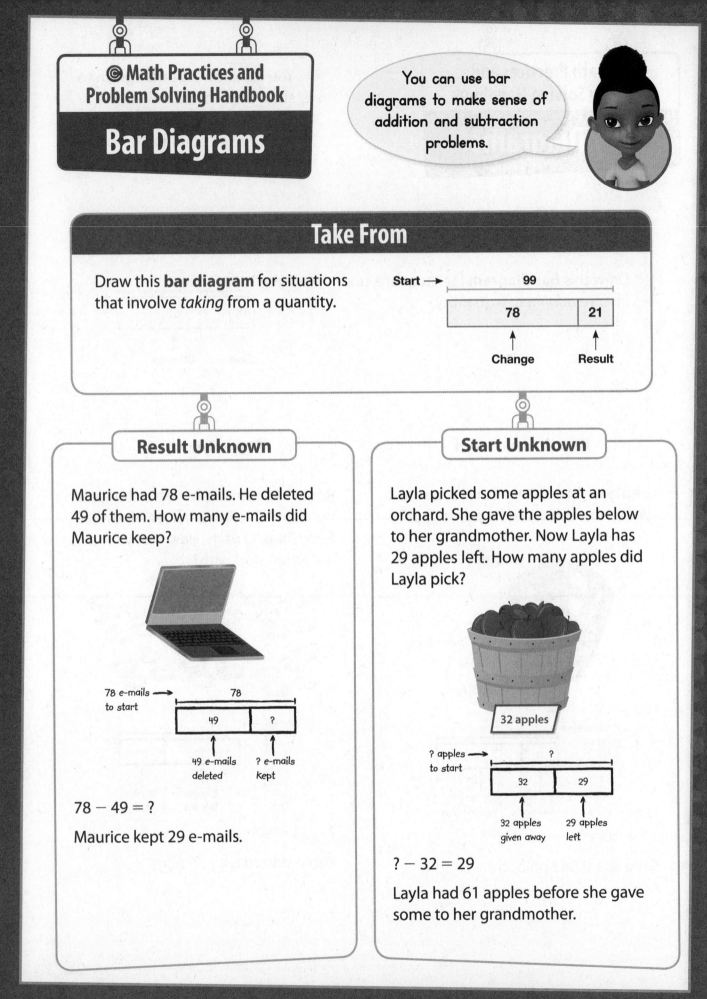

Math Practices and Problem Solving Handbook

Bar Diagrams

You can use bar diagrams to make sense of addition and subtraction problems.

Take From

Draw this **bar diagram** for situations that involve *taking* from a quantity.

Start → | 99 |
| 78 | 21 |
↑ Change   ↑ Result

Result Unknown

Maurice had 78 e-mails. He deleted 49 of them. How many e-mails did Maurice keep?

78 e-mails to start → | 78 |
| 49 | ? |
↑ 49 e-mails deleted   ↑ ? e-mails kept

$78 - 49 = ?$

Maurice kept 29 e-mails.

Start Unknown

Layla picked some apples at an orchard. She gave the apples below to her grandmother. Now Layla has 29 apples left. How many apples did Layla pick?

32 apples

? apples to start → | ? |
| 32 | 29 |
↑ 32 apples given away   ↑ 29 apples left

$? - 32 = 29$

Layla had 61 apples before she gave some to her grandmother.

The **bar diagrams** on this page can help you make sense of more addition and subtraction situations.

Put Together/Take Apart

Draw this **bar diagram** for situations that involve *putting together* or *taking apart* quantities.

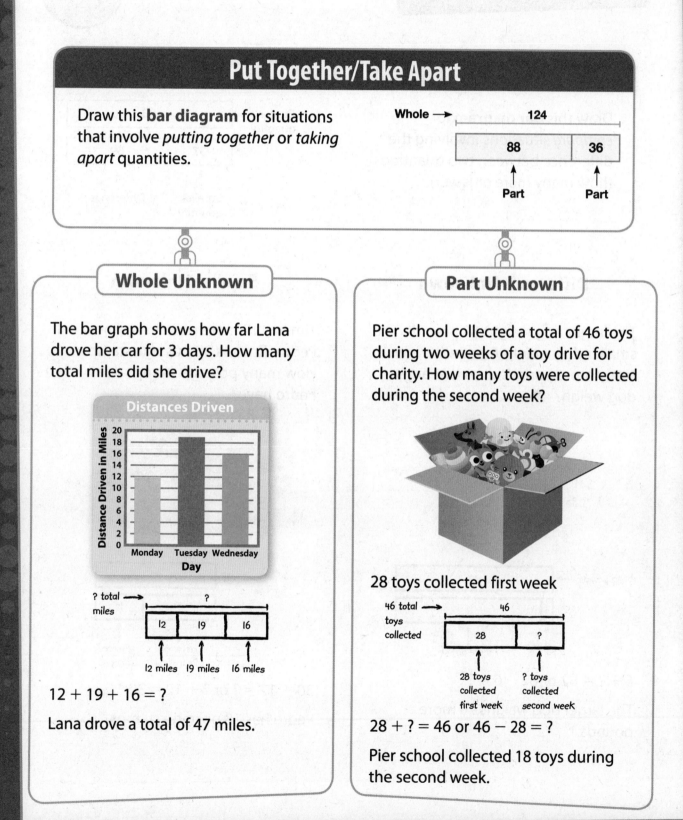

Whole → 124

| 88 | 36 |

↑ Part   ↑ Part

Whole Unknown

The bar graph shows how far Lana drove her car for 3 days. How many total miles did she drive?

Distances Driven

Distance Driven in Miles

20 18 16 14 12 10 8 6 4 2 0

Monday Tuesday Wednesday
Day

? total → miles

| 12 | 19 | 16 |

↑ 12 miles   ↑ 19 miles   ↑ 16 miles

12 + 19 + 16 = ?

Lana drove a total of 47 miles.

Part Unknown

Pier school collected a total of 46 toys during two weeks of a toy drive for charity. How many toys were collected during the second week?

28 toys collected first week

46 total → toys collected

| 28 | ? |

↑ 28 toys collected first week   ↑ ? toys collected second week

28 + ? = 46 or 46 − 28 = ?

Pier school collected 18 toys during the second week.

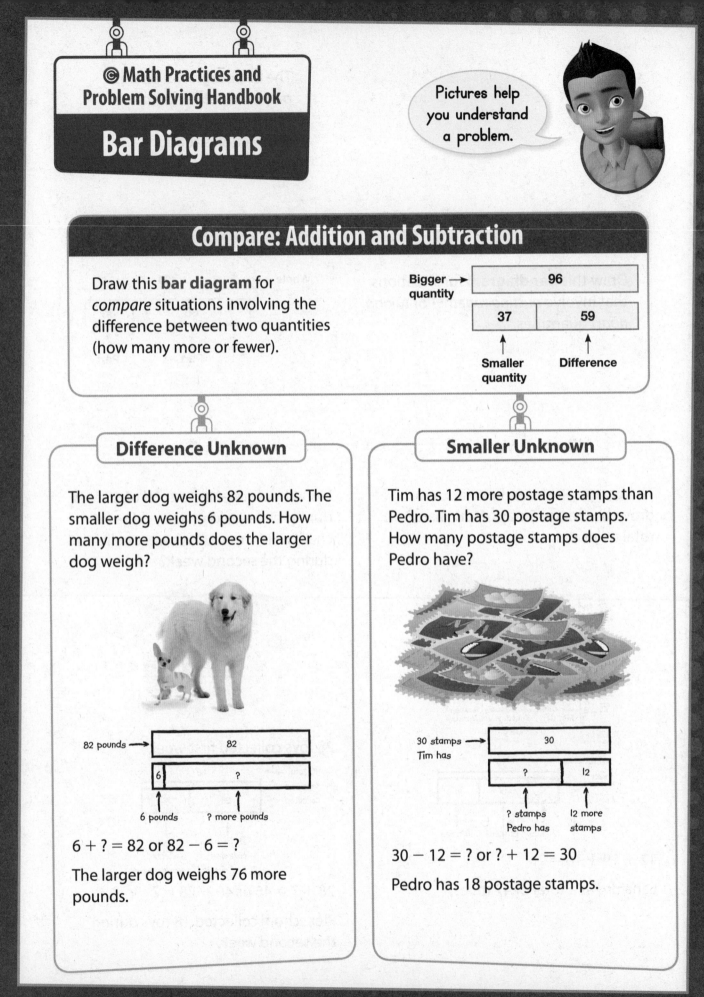

Math Practices and Problem Solving Handbook

Bar Diagrams

Pictures help you understand a problem.

Compare: Addition and Subtraction

Draw this **bar diagram** for *compare* situations involving the difference between two quantities (how many more or fewer).

Bigger quantity → | 96 |

| 37 | 59 |

↑ Smaller quantity   ↑ Difference

Difference Unknown

The larger dog weighs 82 pounds. The smaller dog weighs 6 pounds. How many more pounds does the larger dog weigh?

82 pounds → | 82 |

| 6 | ? |

↑ 6 pounds   ↑ ? more pounds

$6 + ? = 82$ or $82 - 6 = ?$

The larger dog weighs 76 more pounds.

Smaller Unknown

Tim has 12 more postage stamps than Pedro. Tim has 30 postage stamps. How many postage stamps does Pedro have?

30 stamps Tim has → | 30 |

| ? | 12 |

↑ ? stamps Pedro has   ↑ 12 more stamps

$30 - 12 = ?$ or $? + 12 = 30$

Pedro has 18 postage stamps.

The **bar diagrams** on this page can help you solve problems involving multiplication and division.

Equal Groups: Multiplication and Division

Draw this **bar diagram** for situations that involve *equal groups*.

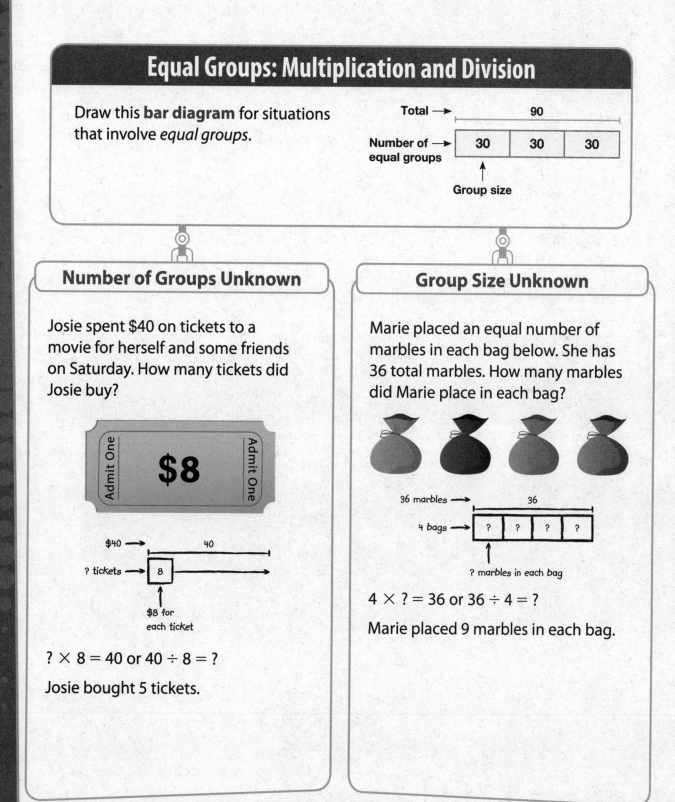

Total → 90

Number of → equal groups 30 | 30 | 30

↑ Group size

Number of Groups Unknown

Josie spent $40 on tickets to a movie for herself and some friends on Saturday. How many tickets did Josie buy?

Admit One **$8** Admit One

$40 →   40
? tickets → 8 →

↑ $8 for each ticket

? × 8 = 40 or 40 ÷ 8 = ?

Josie bought 5 tickets.

Group Size Unknown

Marie placed an equal number of marbles in each bag below. She has 36 total marbles. How many marbles did Marie place in each bag?

36 marbles →   36
4 bags → ? | ? | ? | ?

↑ ? marbles in each bag

4 × ? = 36 or 36 ÷ 4 = ?

Marie placed 9 marbles in each bag.